J
362.29
SHA

Shapiro, Harry.

Facts on drugs and sport.

$11.90

LL
Bea
vg

OK

Design	David West
	Children's Book Design
Editor:	Roger Vlitos
Editorial planning:	Clark Robinson
Illustrator:	Peter Bull
Picture research:	Cecilia Weston-Baker

Photographic Credits:
Cover and pages 8, 9, 12, 25t, 26: Frank Spooner; pages 6, 7: Vanessa Bailey;
page 7: Holford; pages 10, 15b, 25b, 27: Colorsport; pages 11, 13, 16: Robert
Harding; pages 13b, 17b, 21b, 24: Zefa; pages 13b, 14-15, 17b, 23b, 28, 29:
Rex Features; pages 14, 22: Popperfoto; page 19: Science Photo Library;
page 20: Shipianek; page 21b: Associated Press; page 23b: News of the
World; pages 4-5, 27b: J. Allan Cash; pages 4-5: Daley Thompson.

Printed in Belgium

*First published in the United
States in 1989 by*
Franklin Watts
387 Park Avenue South
New York, NY 10016

Shapiro, Harry.
    Facts on drugs and sports / by Harry Shapiro
       p.   cm.
    Includes index.
    Summary: Discusses how athletes use drugs from steroids to diuretics
how these drugs affect the body, and what risks are involved.
    ISBN 0-531-10823-6
    1. Doping in sports--Juvenile literature. [1. Athletes--Drug use. 2. Drug
abuse.] I. Title. II. Title: Drugs and sports.
RC1230.T95 1989
615'.7'085796--dc20   89-8094
                                           CIP
                                           AC

Facts on

Drugs
and
Sport

Harry Shapiro

FRANKLIN WATTS
New York · London · Toronto · Sydney

CONTENTS

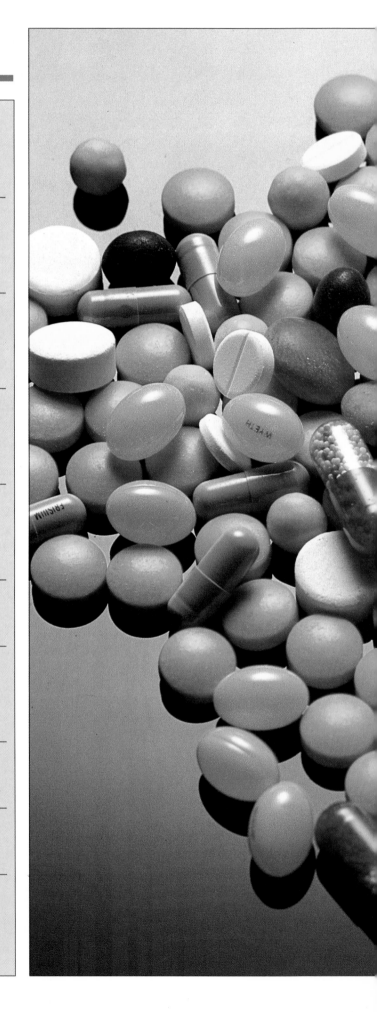

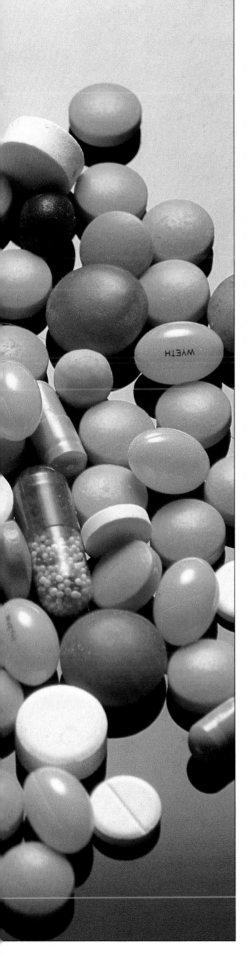

Most people take part in sports for fun and relaxation. But professional sports are taken much more seriously, especially athletics, snooker and football. A lot of money is invested in sport by sponsors, television companies and those who make sports equipment. In many ways, sports are a business and the rewards for coming out on top can be very great.

Top sports personalities are not only famous worldwide, many of them can earn large amounts of money. But the difference between gaining fame and fortune and being forgotten can be very small. For a runner, it might be as little as one tenth of a second. With so much to gain, and such a fine line between success and failure, some sportsmen and sportswomen will do anything to win – including taking drugs.

Most people regard drug taking to improve performance as cheating. Those in charge of sports are determined to try and stop it. They fear that drugs will destroy fair competition. But how can the authorities persuade sportsmen and sportswomen not to take them when the prizes for winning are so great? And how can they prevent a drug trade worth billions of dollars to drug dealers?

WHAT DRUGS ARE USED?

Many kinds of drugs are used by athletes competing in sports all over the world. Some are used to build muscles or give the athlete extra energy. Others kill the pain of injuries or calm nerves. Most of these drugs have proper medical uses. Others are the same as illegal drugs that are taken by drug addicts. All of these drugs can cause serious health problems if they are misused on a regular basis in high doses or without proper medical supervision; and most of them are banned by sporting authorities worldwide. There are five main groups of drugs which some people claim have been taken by athletes and that are banned in sports: anabolic steroids and hormone growth drugs, stimulants, beta-blockers, narcotic analgesics and diuretics.

WHAT THEY CAN DO

Anabolic steroids and hormone growth drugs (which some people call HGDs) make muscles grow larger, and so are used by bodybuilders, weightlifters and people in throwing events, such as discus and javelin. Stimulants increase alertness and heartbeat and reduce tiredness, giving a feeling of elation and confidence. They can also increase aggression and competitiveness. Some people abuse them in sport in an attempt to increase speed and endurance. Beta-blockers steady shaking hands. Alcohol and tranquilizers are used by some athletes for the same purpose. They can be a help in all sports, particularly those requiring good coordination, such as archery, shooting and pool. Narcotic analgesics kill pain, and they may enable players of contact sports to continue playing even

BLOOD DOPING
Extra blood is injected into the person's veins to increase the red blood cells and oxygen in the bloodstream. In this way a competitor tries to increase the stamina level of muscles.

after being injured. They may be taken by ice hockey or football players. Diuretics help the body to lose water, and have been used by boxers and tennis players who wish to lose weight.

THE FIRST DRUGS

Athletes in Ancient Egypt drank a mixture of boiled donkey hoof, rose petals and rosehips, believing it would make them winners. The winner of the 200 meters at the Olympic Games of 668 BC in Ancient Greece used a special diet of figs.

STIMULANTS
Taken to speed up the central nervous system.

BETA-BLOCKERS
Taken to slow down the heart rate and control stress and anxiety.

STEROIDS
Injected into the muscles or taken as tablets in an attempt to build leg, arm and chest muscles.

NARCOTIC ANALGESICS AND CORTICOSTEROIDS
Drugs that are injected to kill pain at the site of injury or swallowed as tablets.

WHAT DRUGS ARE USED?

ANABOLIC STEROIDS

Steroids make up one type of hormone normally found in the body. There are male hormones and female hormones. It is the male hormones that make men hairier than women and give them deeper voices. The steroids used in sports resemble male hormones. "Anabolic" means to build up – in this case to build up muscles. Bodybuilders use anabolic steroids in order to look good in competitions. But for scientific reasons, big muscles do not necessarily mean extra strength.

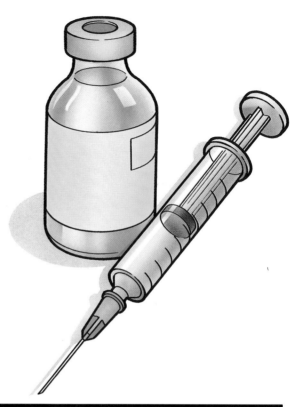

STIMULANTS

The main stimulants used in sports are cocaine, amphetamine and drugs called sympathominetic amines. All are banned in sports. Stimulants make you feel full of energy and confidence. They can also make you feel more aggressive. Amphetamine has been abused by cyclists, who need lots of stamina. Cocaine has been used by American football and basketball players to make them more competitive. Ephedrine is present in low doses in preparations used to relieve the symptoms of colds.

WHAT DRUGS ARE USED?

NARCOTIC ANALGESICS

Analgesics are painkillers, such as aspirin and acetaminophen. But these are very mild drugs. Narcotic analgesics are much stronger and much more dangerous. They include drugs such as heroin and morphine, and all are controlled by law. They are also banned in sports. They are not commonly used by sports people because they make you feel very drowsy and sleepy. For painkilling, an athlete might sometimes have an injection of corticosteroid, but such injections are restricted to the treatment of specific ailments, such as an old injury.

BETA-BLOCKERS

Beta-blockers are drugs normally only prescribed by doctors for people with high blood pressure or heart problems. They help calm you down and relieve stress. Pool players, archers and those who shoot in competition all need steady hands and cool nerves. It is rumored that some have taken beta-blockers for this reason. Beta-blockers are not allowed in certain sports, particularly those in which their use might give an advantage. Alcohol is restricted in some sports such as motor racing. However, most athletes avoid alcoholic drinks before competition because they can affect concentration and judgment.

WHY USE THEM?

Sports are big business for some of the athletes involved. As a result, some are desperate to win because they want a share of the fortune and fame. If they believe that others in their event or match might have taken drugs, they will think they are at a disadvantage unless they take drugs as well. They convince themselves that they need to take drugs in order to perform better. By no means do all sports people take drugs. Most want to see drugs banned and kept right out of sports, and not just because drugs give sports a bad name. Sports can be enjoyed by everyone and successful sports people are the heroes of young people. Knowing an athlete uses drugs would set a poor example and make people think less of him or her. We would never know if it was the athlete or the drug that won the race.

THE DESIRE TO WIN

Without the desire to win, no competitor can succeed. Training and practice take hours every day for months or years on end. There may be injuries. But he or she battles through, all for the chance to rush through the tape ahead of everyone else, score the winning goal, or hold up that winner's trophy.

THE MONEY INVOLVED

Winning in sports has always been important to those taking part. But nowadays, there is something more — very large amounts of money. Some people claim that drug abuse in sports increases as the rewards get larger. The successful athlete, for example, can expect to receive fees for:

* competing in special meets
* using (and therefore advertising) a particular brand of sports goods
* giving interviews to newspapers
* publishing a book
* making guest appearances on television
* opening stores, fairs, supermarkets, and so on. Professional football players and other players of team sports are even "sold" for large sums to other sides; part of this "transfer fee" often goes to the player.

WHY USE THEM?

BETTER COMPETITION?

In athletics, men and women are throwing further and running faster. But the winning margins are getting smaller. The tiniest fraction of a second may be all that separates first from second in a sprint. When things get that close, some athletes will consider doing anything to give themselves an edge over their rivals. As one coach said, "Drugs will put you a yard ahead."

In team sports, competition for a place on the starting team is getting fiercer as more people become professionals and get more money for doing so. A player is under pressure not only to beat the other team but also to stay in the team and play better than his or her teammates. Some think that drugs are the answer.

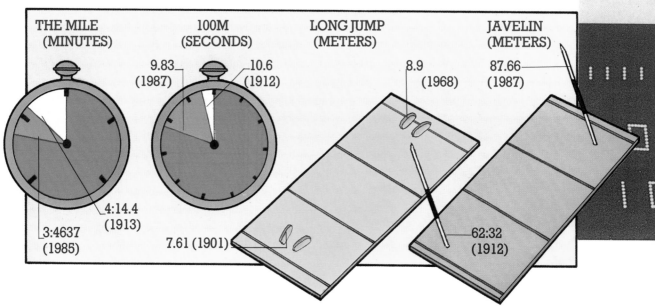

THE MILE (MINUTES)	100M (SECONDS)	LONG JUMP (METERS)	JAVELIN (METERS)

9.83 (1987)   10.6 (1912)

8.9 (1968)

87.66 (1987)

4:14.4 (1913)

3:4637 (1985)

7.61 (1901)

62:32 (1912)

SECOND ISN'T GOOD ENOUGH

In international sports, people may train for years to be able to run fast in one particular race, or play well in one particular match. They have to time their fitness to the day so that they do the very best they can. They may need to win one competition after another to get to the top. When they reach important competitions such as the Olympics, the pressure to succeed is strong, and the fear of letting down their team and country is intense. There are no second chances. Failure makes all the time and effort put into training seem worthless.

IS IT CHEATING?

Most people agree that taking drugs to perform better in sports is cheating. They think it is unfair to those who do not take drugs. If a drug gives a runner an invisible head start, that surely means he is cheating! But athletes can do other things to perform well, and not every athlete is able to take advantage of these things. For instance, some athletes have better equipment than others or can go abroad for training because it is paid for by a sponsor. Other athletes can afford better training facilities because they are already successful. Some athletes are put on special vitamin diets, and some have their training worked out scientifically, using expensive equipment. Are these athletes "cheating"? Are athletes who take drugs so different? According to the rules they are.

The rules about drugs and sports can seem confusing. You can have an alcoholic drink to relax before some sports – but not in others. You can take some pain-killers but not codeine, which is a narcotic analgesic. Caffeine, a stimulant, is banned only in high doses. These rules are made to stop cheating. Many have also come about to protect the athletes from dangerous drugs. Because the rewards are so great, some people take foolish risks. The rules safeguard sports and competitors.

TRAINING ADVANTAGE

Among professional sports people, more time and work is spent training than taking part in an event. Athletes do not only take drugs to give themselves an advantage over others when they are competing; drugs are also taken to give an advantage in training. For example, drugs may allow an athlete to train for a longer time before feeling tiredness or pain. Taking drugs during training is as unfair as taking them when performing. It is also difficult to prove that someone has taken drugs when training because he or she can stop taking them before an event where they might be tested.

ACCIDENTAL DRUGS

Some athletes have to take remedies for hay fever in the summer: many of these contain such banned substances as ephedrine, which show up in drug test results. This happened to British sprinter Lynford Christie (right) when he won a medal in the 1988 Olympics. He was able to prove his innocence, but when this is not possible, all the hard work of training could turn out to be for nothing. Athletes must therefore be very wary, taking advice from the experts.

THE DANGERS OF DRUGS

There is no such thing as a safe drug. All drugs can cause problems if they are misused. The greatest risks occur where drugs are used in high doses. Possible damage to health depends on:

* The person's health before he or she started using drugs.
* Whether the drug has been mixed with other things to bulk up the quantity. This extra substance may be chalk, milk powder or even poison.
* Whether different drugs are being taken together.
* Whether drugs are being injected (there is the danger of AIDS).
* The long-term effect the drug has on the body.

There are various risks if you use drugs. The side-effects differ from one person to another.

STIMULANTS

Stimulants do not create energy – they take it from what the body has already. Eventually, users feel exhausted and washed out. These drugs also kill your appetite. When you stop taking them, severe depression can set in. They are also extremely addictive.

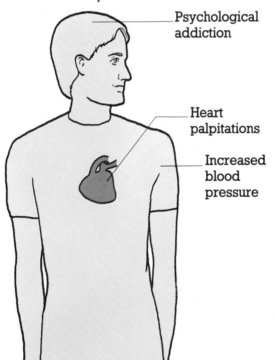

Psychological addiction

Heart palpitations

Increased blood pressure

NARCOTIC ANALGESICS

These drugs have the opposite effect to stimulants; they slow you down. Heavy and regular users are generally drowsy. Heroin, the best known drug of this group, is physically addictive. While these drugs mask pain, they can lead to further damage of the body.

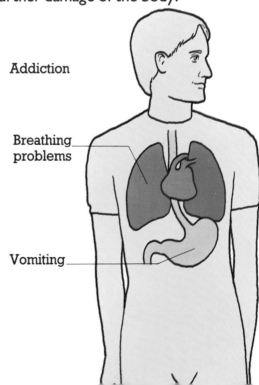

Addiction

Breathing problems

Vomiting

BLOOD DOPING

Athletes are sometimes injected with extra blood to increase oxygen to the blood cells. This gives them more energy and stamina. The blood is either the athlete's own, taken some time before and later re-injected, or someone else's. It can be a risky business. Someone else's blood might be contaminated (perhaps with AIDS or the liver disease hepatitis). Or the injecting equipment might not be sterile which could cause infection or blood poisoning. The body may even reject the new blood, resulting in anemia.

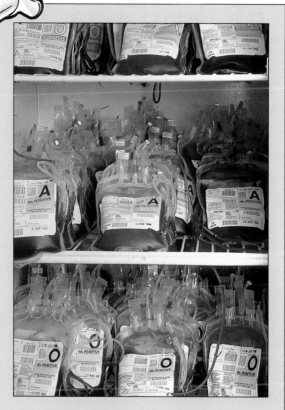

BETA-BLOCKERS

People who are very fit often have slow heart rates. Beta-blockers – used for treating high blood pressure – slow down the heart so it can be dangerous for sports people to use them. They can also cause breathing difficulties.

STEROIDS

Many athletes use a number of steroids in combination, especially during training. Most of the medical uses involve one or two steroids given in low doses over a short period of time. But there are risks of possible side effects.

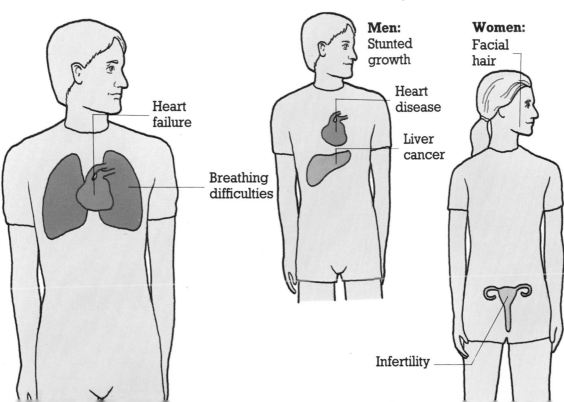

Heart
failure

Breathing
difficulties

Men:
Stunted
growth

Heart
disease

Liver
cancer

Women:
Facial
hair

Infertility

THE DANGERS OF DRUGS

Cocaine, amphetamine, narcotic analgesics and steroids can all be injected into the body. This is the most dangerous way of using drugs. Injections into veins, muscles or just under the skin are all equally dangerous. The risks can be very high, especially if needles are shared or injected by untrained people, which is likely if the drugs are being taken in secret. Such risks include infection with the HIV virus, which can lead to AIDS; infection with hepatitis (a form of liver disease), blood poisoning and gangrene (which could even result in the amputation of limbs).

Another danger of taking these banned drugs is addiction. The greatest risk of physical drug addiction comes from regular use of narcotic analgesics, particularly heroin. When people stop using the drug, they feel very ill until they start using it again. These feelings include sickness, sweating and stomach cramps. The most immediate danger is overdosing. When this happens the body slows down so much that it stops altogether. If breathing stops, the person dies. Another serious danger also comes from using drugs in a way they were never meant to be used. Most drugs were designed only to be taken when something has gone wrong. They were not meant to improve the physical condition of somebody who is healthy. If they are misused in this way, they can have unwanted side-effects. Over a period of time the drugs can start to cause serious damage.

LEN BIAS

When people take stimulants their hearts beat faster and their blood pressure rises. Stimulants are especially dangerous when doing hard exercise – there is a risk of a heart attack. The problem is that people on stimulants think they can keep going and they push their bodies too far. A British cyclist, Tommy Simpson, and Len Bias, an American basketball player, both died in this way.

AMERICAN FOOTBALL

Some sports, such as American football, are very violent. They are played by very strong and heavy people. Every sports person involved in such a sport is likely to be injured at some time or other. Players may feel pressured to go on playing, even after they have been hurt, because of the money involved and the importance attached to winning. Painkillers can enable players to go on, but only by covering up the natural pain that is telling the player that something is very wrong.

THE DANGERS OF DRUGS

There are many risks associated with long-term use of steroids. These include:

* Temporary liver problems
* More serious, but rare, liver and kidney cancer
* Increased blood pressure
* In young people, steroids can stunt growth by "closing" the ends of bones where growth normally takes place
* There is some evidence of "steroid madness", possibly connected with the increased aggressiveness caused by taking these drugs
* Other possible mental problems include confusion, hallucinations (seeing imaginary things) and depression

AGAINST THE LAW

Many of the drugs banned in sports are also illegal. It is against the law to possess or sell heroin, cocaine or amphetamines except under the guidance of a medical doctor.

The penalty in America for selling heroin or cocaine is very harsh. You could go to prison and pay a very heavy fine just for having it in your possession. It is also against the law to sell unprescribed steroids.

SEXUAL SIDE-EFFECTS

Taking steroids can cause changes in a person's maleness or femaleness. In men there is a possibility of developing breasts. Steroids may also cause male infertility or an inability to have sexual intercourse. This may or may not return to normal after the drug is stopped. In women, steroids cause irregular periods and possible infertility. Appearance of male features, such as a deep voice, facial hair, baldness and smaller breasts, also occurs.

'I WAS TURNING INTO A MAN'

WHAT IS BEING DONE?

Sports authorities at both national and international levels all agree that drug abuse is sport's major problem. They believe fair play is ruined by cheats who take drugs. They realize that this gives sport a bad image. They also feel that they have to protect athletes. They have taken responsibility for the detection of drugs used by athletes, and for the punishment of anyone involved; competitors, trainers and coaches. To do this they test samples of urine from competitors. At the last Olympic Games urine samples were taken from every athlete. The winners of the events had their samples tested afterwards. Some competitors were found to have taken banned drugs. They were forced to give their medals back and leave the games in disgrace.

TESTING

Attempts to stop drug abuse in sports have been going on for more than 30 years. In the mid-1960s, France and Belgium introduced laws to try to stop bicyclists from using amphetamine. Some competitors were tested in 1968 at the Grenoble Winter Olympic Games, but proper testing did not begin until the Munich Olympics of 1972. A reliable test for steroids was not available until 1973. In 1976, at the Montreal Olympic Games, Danuta Rosari from Poland became the first Olympic athlete to be banned for using steroids.

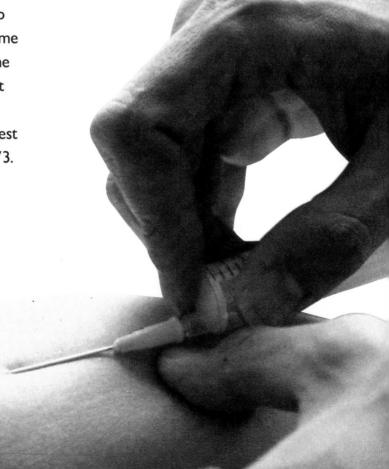

IN THE LAB

When a drug is taken, some of it passes into the bloodstream and then into urine. Using special equipment, scientists can tell which drug or drugs have been taken – and how much – by analysing a sample of urine provided by the athlete. The result can be confirmed by repeating the test on a second sample of urine that has been kept sealed.

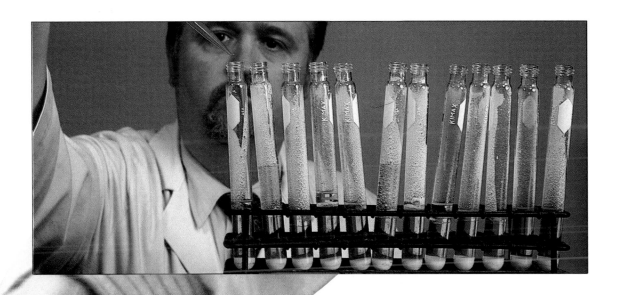

STOPPING THE TRADE

Stopping the illegal trade in drugs is the job of police and Customs officials throughout the world. It is a very expensive operation involving specially-trained officers working undercover and using helicopters, boats and sniffer dogs. They face highly organised gangs who will stop at nothing to satisfy the demand for drugs. They are also battling against those sports people who themselves sell drugs to other people. David Jenkins, the runner, admitted taking part in this illegal trade in banned drugs and to supplying athletes with them. Many police officers believe they are fighting an international battle. They do not think they are winning.

WHAT IS BEING DONE?

SHAMING THE OFFENDERS

Some drug takers and drug dealers do get caught. In 1987, Dwight Gooden, a successful pitcher for the New York Mets, failed a routine drugs test. The management suggested that he go for rehabilitation before they would let him pitch again. Less fortunate was Len Bias, an All-American star center from the University of Maryland, who died suddenly from a cocaine overdose.

Seven athletes were caught taking drugs at the Olympics in Seoul in 1988. They were immediately disqualified from the competition. Any medals they had won were taken away. One of these was the Canadian sprinter Ben Johnson, and his expulsion from the games made worldwide headlines. Also in 1988, Angel Myers, a member of the US Swim Team, was disqualified for using steroids. Others have been fined or suspended from competition.

Ben Johnson faces the press; use of drugs can mean disgrace in the world of sport.

DRUG-FREE WINNING

To win an event is to prove that you have the greatest skill, health and fitness. Winning results from hard work and training. It is something that should give a sense of pride and achievement. The pleasure of winning comes from knowing that the trophy is deserved. Sports people are being encouraged to keep this in mind. Taking drugs reduces the pleasure of sport. If you take drugs, the achievement is not completely your own.

DIET

A good diet is important for everyone's physical well-being. Many athletes have special diets to give them energy or to provide them with the kinds of food they need to build up muscles. Eating a special diet brings out the natural ability of an athlete. It is very different from taking artificial drugs. Drugs damage health instead of improving it.

ANTI-DRUGS

Many star names in the sports world have spoken out against the use of drugs in sports. By doing so, they hope to shame those who take drugs. They also hope to stop young people from copying their "heroes". They want to make it clear that taking drugs is cheating, and they want to warn about the serious dangers of taking drugs. They know, better than anyone, that sports people do not need drugs – and neither does anybody else! As Florence Griffith Joyner, the Olympic gold-medalist, known as "the fastest woman alive", has said, "I don't think a person has to use drugs. There is no substitute for hard work." Many of the world's finest athletes from all sports agree with her and have joined the campaign to keep sport free of drugs.

DRUG-FREE, AND PROUD

The attitude to drug taking in sports can be summed up in the words of two famous British athletes: "We might be heading for the day when you have to take drugs just to be competitive. We must never allow that to happen." – Roger Black, British sprint champion, at the 1986 Commonwealth and European Games.

"Those competitors who take drugs are going against the whole spirit of the Olympic Games. They are cheats." – Sebastian Coe, Olympic Champion.

PUBLICITY

Issues such as drug taking are very serious. One of the best ways to make people understand this is through publicity. All over the world there are organisations responsible for the control of drugs in sports. These organisations arrange information campaigns to educate people about the dangers of drug taking. News on television and in newspapers about drug taking also helps to increase publicity. Governments and sports organisations are planning to increase the publicity about drugs in sport. This publicity will include sports people talking on television and radio, as well as poster campaigns, shirts and buttons.

SPORTS AUTHORITIES

Sports authorities like the International Olympic Committee (IOC), the International Amateur Athletics Federation (IAAF) and the Athletics Congress of USA exist to detect the presence of drugs in athletes. The IOC has a list of banned drugs which has become the standard for many sports. It also bans some methods of improving performance besides drug taking, such as blood-doping.

Banned drugs and methods include:

* All stimulants, such as cocaine, amphetamine, ephedrine and caffeine (in high quantities)
* Narcotic analgesics, such as heroin, morphine and codeine
* Anabolic steroids and the male sex hormone testosterone
* Growth hormones
* Beta-blockers
* Diuretics
* Blood doping techniques

The IOC adds the words "and related compounds" at the end of each drug type on the list. This means that any similar drug not actually listed is still banned. Since the 1988 Olympic Games, the IOC has also banned the taking of a drug that was not banned in order to hide the presence of a drug that was. In other words, this covers any future attempt to use another drug like Probenecid to hide the presence of steroids or any other drug that is banned by the IOC.

WHERE YOU CAN GET FURTHER INFORMATION

The International Olympic Committee (IOC), Chateau de Vidy, 1007 Lausanne, Switzerland

You can get copies of the IOC list of banned drugs from this address, and a list of medication which is safe to take with guidance.

Athletics Congress of USA, P.O. Box 120, Indianapolis, Indiana, A6206, 01020, USA

The IAAF is the international governing body for track and field athletics. It publishes several booklets about the dangers of drug abuse (for example, Save the Future, Save Yourself), procedures for drug testing and control (Doping Control Regulations) and the proper diet control for athletes (Too Thin to Win).

Australian Sports Medicine Federation (ASMF), PO Box 243, Kingston, ACT 2604.

The ASMF has developed a series of education programs for the entire sports community, including athletes, coaches and doctors. It produces a Drug Education Resource Kit, which contains videos, booklets, leaflets and posters about the dangers of drug abuse, testing procedures and alternative medications.

Prestel has an Information Paper and Worksheet on Drugs in Sport on page 30000910A.

United States Olympic Committee (USOC), 1750 East Boulder Street, Colorado Springs, Colorado 80909-5760.

The USOC has a telephone hot-line for queries about banned substances and medications. The number is 800 233 0393. The Committee administers testing programs for competitors, coaches and doctors. The National Collegiate Athletic Association (NCAA) administers a program for college athletes.

GLOSSARY

AIDS anti-immune deficiency syndrome, a disease caused by the human HIV virus and contracted through infected body fluids. Can be passed through sexual contact or contaminated hypodermic needles.

anabolic steroid male sex hormone that promotes the growth of muscles. Taken as a drug it results in weight gain but can cause masculinisation in women.

analgesic drug that suppresses pain; examples include aspirin and acetaminophen. In large doses narcotic analgesics, such as morphine, produce unconsciousness; they are also addictive.

beta-blocker drug that slows the heartbeat; used by doctors to treat high blood pressure and the heart disease known as angina. Sometimes taken by sports people for its calming effect.

corticosteroid any of the steroid hormones produced naturally by the adrenal glands. Synthesised, they become drugs such as cortisone. Long-term misuse to deal with stress can cause harmful side-effects.

diuretic drug used in medicine to stimulate the production of urine (thus reducing the amount of fluid in the body). Misuse to control body weight can lead to serious dehydration.

heroin powerful addictive narcotic drug, made from poppies; illegal in most countries.

stimulant general term for any substance that stimulates the body.

Useful addresses

The following organizations should be able to provide you with further information, booklets, brochures or other printed matter:

American College of Sports Medicine
P.O. Box 1440
Indianapolis, Indiana 46206

Athletic Commission of New York State
270 Broadway
New York, New York 10007

National Basketball Association
"Don't Foul Out"
645 Fifth Avenue
New York, New York 10022

National Clearinghouse for Drug Abuse Information
P.O. Box 2345
Kensington, Maryland 20852

National Hockey League Services
Public Relations Department
650 Fifth Avenue
New York, New York 10019

INDEX

PRINTED IN BELGIUM BY
proost
INTERNATIONAL BOOK PRODUCTION